Mastering the CCNP: A Comprehensive Exam Prep Guide

Table of Contents

Chapter 1: Introduction to CCNP Certification

Welcome to Chapter 1 of "Mastering the CCNP: A Comprehensive Exam Prep Guide." In this chapter, we will introduce you to the world of CCNP certification, its benefits, exam format, and help you create a study plan for success. Let's get started!

Section 1: What is CCNP Certification?

CCNP (Cisco Certified Network Professional) is a widely recognized certification offered by Cisco Systems. It validates your advanced knowledge and skills in designing, implementing, and managing complex network solutions. Achieving CCNP certification demonstrates your expertise in routing and switching technologies, WANs, security, and other critical networking concepts.

Section 2: Benefits of CCNP Certification

Earning your CCNP certification offers several advantages:

Enhanced Career Opportunities: CCNP certification opens doors to a wide range of job opportunities, such as network engineer, network administrator, and network consultant. It can also lead to higher-paying positions and career advancement.

Industry Recognition: CCNP is a globally recognized certification, respected by employers and networking professionals worldwide. It serves as a testament to your skills and expertise in the networking field.

Up-to-Date Knowledge: To obtain the CCNP certification, you need to stay updated with the latest networking technologies and best practices. This ensures that you are equipped with the most current knowledge and skills in the industry.

Networking Community: By becoming CCNP certified, you gain access to a vast community of networking professionals. This community provides networking opportunities, resources, and support to help you grow in your career.

Section 3: Understanding the CCNP Exam Format

The CCNP certification consists of multiple exams that you need to pass to obtain the certification. The specific exams may vary depending on the track you choose, such as CCNP Routing and Switching, CCNP Security, or CCNP Data Center. Each exam typically consists of a combination of multiple-choice questions, simulations, and hands-on lab scenarios.

To prepare for the exam, it is crucial to familiarize yourself with the exam topics and objectives outlined by Cisco. These topics serve as a blueprint for your study plan and help you focus on the areas that will be covered in the exam.

Section 4: Creating a Study Plan

To maximize your chances of success, it is essential to create a well-structured study plan. Here are some steps to help you get started:

Assess Your Current Knowledge: Begin by evaluating your existing knowledge and identifying areas that require improvement. This self-assessment will help you gauge the amount of time and effort needed to prepare for the exam effectively.

Set a Realistic Timeline: Determine a timeline for your exam preparation. Consider your schedule, available study hours per day or week, and any other commitments you may have. Setting a realistic timeline will help you stay organized and motivated throughout your preparation journey.

Break Down the Exam Objectives: Divide the exam objectives into manageable sections or chapters. This will enable you to focus on one topic at a time and track your progress effectively.

Study Resources: Gather study materials such as textbooks, online courses, practice exams, and Cisco documentation. Utilize a combination of resources to ensure a well-rounded understanding of the exam topics.

Practice, Practice, Practice: Hands-on practice is crucial for CCNP exam success. Set up a lab environment using virtualization software or physical equipment to gain practical experience with network configurations and troubleshooting.

Review and Reinforce: Regularly review the topics you have studied to reinforce your knowledge. Take practice exams to assess your progress and identify areas that need further attention.

Section 5: Conclusion

In this chapter, we introduced you to CCNP certification, discussed its benefits, explained the exam format, and guided you through creating a study plan. Remember, CCNP certification requires dedication, hands-on practice, and a thorough understanding of networking concepts. Stay focused, follow your study plan, and you'll be well on your way to mastering the CCNP certification.

In the next chapter, we will dive into the fundamentals of routing and switching, providing you with a solid foundation for your CCNP journey.

Chapter 2: Routing and Switching Fundamentals

Welcome to Chapter 2 of "Mastering the CCNP: A Comprehensive Exam Prep Guide." In this chapter, we will explore the fundamentals of routing and switching. We'll cover the OSI model, TCP/IP protocols, IP addressing, subnetting, routing protocols, switching technologies, and IPv6. Let's begin!

Section 1: Understanding the OSI Model

The OSI (Open Systems Interconnection) model is a conceptual framework that helps us understand how network protocols interact and communicate. It consists of seven layers:

Physical Layer: This layer deals with the physical transmission of data over the network, including cables, connectors, and electrical signals.

Data Link Layer: The data link layer provides error-free transmission of data between adjacent network nodes. It includes protocols like Ethernet and MAC addresses.

Network Layer: The network layer handles the logical addressing and routing of data packets. IP (Internet Protocol) is a key protocol at this layer.

Transport Layer: The transport layer ensures reliable delivery of data by segmenting and reassembling data into packets. TCP (Transmission Control Protocol) and UDP (User Datagram Protocol) operate at this layer.

Session Layer: The session layer establishes, maintains, and terminates communication sessions between devices. It manages session synchronization and checkpoints.

Presentation Layer: The presentation layer deals with data formatting, encryption, and compression. It ensures that data is presented correctly for the application layer.

Application Layer: The application layer provides network services to user applications, such as email, web browsing, and file transfer.

Section 2: TCP/IP Protocols

TCP/IP is the protocol suite used for communication over the Internet. It consists of several protocols, including:

Internet Protocol (IP): IP is responsible for addressing and routing packets across different networks. IPv4 and IPv6 are the two main versions of IP.

Transmission Control Protocol (TCP): TCP provides reliable, connection-oriented data delivery. It guarantees packet delivery, in order, with error detection and correction.

User Datagram Protocol (UDP): UDP is a connectionless protocol that offers fast, unreliable data delivery. It is suitable for real-time applications like video streaming and VoIP.

Internet Control Message Protocol (ICMP): ICMP facilitates the exchange of error messages and operational information between network devices. It is commonly used for diagnostics and troubleshooting.

Section 3: IP Addressing and Subnetting

IP addresses are unique numerical identifiers assigned to devices on a network. They can be IPv4 or IPv6 addresses. IPv4 addresses consist of four sets of numbers (e.g., 192.168.0.1), while IPv6 addresses are longer and written in hexadecimal format.

Subnetting allows us to divide a network into smaller subnetworks for efficient address allocation. It involves creating a network address and host address portion within an IP address. Subnet masks are used to determine the network and host portions.

Section 4: Routing Protocols

Routing protocols enable routers to exchange routing information and make decisions on the best paths for packet forwarding. Some common routing protocols include:

Routing Information Protocol (RIP): RIP is a distance vector routing protocol that uses hop count as a metric. It is suitable for small networks.

Open Shortest Path First (OSPF): OSPF is a link-state routing protocol that calculates the shortest path based on network topology. It is widely used in large networks.

Enhanced Interior Gateway Routing Protocol (EIGRP): EIGRP is a hybrid routing protocol that combines characteristics of both distance vector and link-state protocols. It is a Cisco proprietary protocol.

Border Gateway Protocol (BGP): BGP is an exterior gateway protocol used for routing between autonomous systems (AS). It is primarily used in large-scale enterprise and ISP networks.

Section 5: Switching Technologies

Switches are essential networking devices that enable devices within a network to communicate with each other. Some key switching technologies include:

Virtual LANs (VLANs): VLANs allow you to logically segment a network, grouping devices into separate broadcast domains regardless of their physical location.

Spanning Tree Protocol (STP): STP prevents loops in Ethernet networks by creating a loop-free topology. It ensures redundant links are blocked while maintaining network connectivity.

EtherChannel: EtherChannel is a technology that allows you to aggregate multiple physical links into a single logical link. It increases bandwidth and provides redundancy.

Section 6: IPv6 Fundamentals

IPv6 is the next-generation IP addressing protocol. It offers a larger address space, improved security, and additional features. Some key aspects of IPv6 include:

Address Format: IPv6 addresses are 128 bits long, written in hexadecimal format with colons separating each group of four digits.

Address Types: IPv6 introduces different types of addresses, including unicast, multicast, and anycast addresses.

Address Allocation: IPv6 addresses are allocated differently than IPv4 addresses. Internet service providers and organizations receive blocks of IPv6 addresses from regional registries.

Transition Mechanisms: IPv6 transition mechanisms help with the coexistence and migration from IPv4 to IPv6. These include tunneling, dual-stack implementation, and translation techniques.

Section 7: Conclusion

In this chapter, we explored the fundamentals of routing and switching. We discussed the OSI model, TCP/IP protocols, IP addressing, subnetting, routing protocols, switching technologies, and IPv6. Building a strong foundation in these concepts is crucial for your CCNP journey.

In the next chapter, we will delve into the implementation and management of EIGRP, a key routing protocol. We will cover its configuration, optimization, troubleshooting, and security aspects.

Chapter 3: Implementing and Managing EIGRP

Welcome to Chapter 3 of "Mastering the CCNP: A Comprehensive Exam Prep Guide." In this chapter, we will focus on EIGRP (Enhanced Interior Gateway Routing Protocol). We will explore its implementation, management, advanced features, optimization techniques, troubleshooting, and security aspects. Let's dive in!

Section 1: EIGRP Overview and Basic Configuration

EIGRP is a Cisco proprietary routing protocol known for its efficient use of bandwidth and fast convergence. It uses a hybrid approach, incorporating aspects of both distance vector and link-state routing protocols. Let's cover the basics of EIGRP configuration:

Enable EIGRP: Start by enabling EIGRP on your Cisco router using the "router eigrp" command in global configuration mode.

Define Autonomous System (AS): Assign a unique Autonomous System number (AS) to your EIGRP configuration using the "router eigrp <AS number>" command.

Network Advertisement: Specify the networks you want to advertise using the "network <network address>" command under the router eigrp configuration mode. This informs EIGRP which interfaces should participate in routing.

Fine-tuning Metrics: By default, EIGRP uses bandwidth and delay as metrics to calculate the best path. You can modify these metrics using the "metric weights" command to influence path selection.

Section 2: EIGRP Advanced Features and Optimization

EIGRP offers several advanced features and optimization techniques to enhance its functionality and improve network performance. Here are some important aspects to explore:

EIGRP Authentication: Implement authentication to secure EIGRP routing updates exchanged between routers. Use the "authentication" command under the router eigrp configuration mode to enable authentication and specify a key.

Route Summarization: Reduce the size of routing tables and improve network efficiency by implementing route summarization. Use the "summary-address" command to configure summarization on an EIGRP router.

EIGRP Stub Routing: Implement EIGRP stub routing to minimize resource usage on remote sites. Stub routers will only advertise default routes or a limited subset of routes, reducing unnecessary updates.

Load Balancing: EIGRP supports load balancing across multiple paths to maximize bandwidth utilization. You can enable equal-cost load balancing using the "maximum-paths" command under the router eigrp configuration mode.

Section 3: Troubleshooting EIGRP Issues

Troubleshooting is a critical skill for network professionals. Let's explore some common EIGRP issues and their troubleshooting techniques:

Neighbor Adjacency Issues: If EIGRP neighbors fail to form an adjacency, verify that they have the same AS number, the interfaces are in the correct EIGRP configuration, and there are no network connectivity or authentication issues.

Routing Loops: EIGRP employs loop prevention mechanisms, but misconfigurations or incorrect metric calculations can still lead to routing loops. Verify the EIGRP configurations, metric settings, and routing tables to identify and resolve the loop issue.

Unequal Load Balancing: If load balancing across multiple paths is not working as expected, check the maximum-paths setting, verify that equal-cost routes are available, and ensure there are no interface or routing issues.

Route Redistribution: When redistributing routes from other routing protocols into EIGRP or vice versa, ensure that the redistribution configurations and filtering mechanisms are correctly set up. Verify the redistribution statements and access-lists for any misconfigurations.

Section 4: EIGRP Authentication and Security

To ensure the security of EIGRP routing updates and prevent unauthorized access, you can implement authentication and encryption techniques. Here are the key security aspects to consider:

Authentication Methods: EIGRP supports several authentication methods, including simple password authentication and Message Digest Algorithm 5 (MD5) authentication. Choose a suitable authentication method and configure it on all participating routers.

Authentication Key Chains: Key chains provide enhanced security by rotating authentication keys at specified intervals. Implement key chains using the "key chain" and "key" commands under the router eigrp configuration mode.

IPsec Encryption: For additional security, you can encrypt EIGRP traffic using IPsec (Internet Protocol Security) protocols such as AH (Authentication Header) and ESP (Encapsulating Security Payload). IPsec provides confidentiality, integrity, and authentication.

Section 5: Conclusion

In this chapter, we explored the implementation and management of EIGRP. We covered its basic configuration, advanced features, optimization techniques, troubleshooting methods, and security aspects. Understanding these topics is crucial for mastering EIGRP and achieving success in the CCNP exam.

In the next chapter, we will delve into the implementation and management of OSPF (Open Shortest Path First), another important routing protocol. We will discuss OSPF configuration, area types, optimization, troubleshooting, and security considerations.

Chapter 4: Implementing and Managing OSPF

Welcome to Chapter 4 of "Mastering the CCNP: A Comprehensive Exam Prep Guide." In this chapter, we will focus on OSPF (Open Shortest Path First), a widely used link-state routing protocol. We will cover OSPF basics, area types, configuration, optimization, troubleshooting, and security considerations. Let's get started!

Section 1: OSPF Basics and Terminology

OSPF is an interior gateway protocol that uses a link-state database to calculate the shortest path for packet forwarding. Understanding OSPF basics and terminology is essential. Here are the key concepts:

Areas: OSPF networks are divided into areas, each identified by a unique area ID. Areas provide hierarchical structure, reducing routing table size and improving scalability.

Router Types: OSPF defines various router types, including the internal router, which resides entirely within an area, and the backbone router, which connects multiple areas.

Link-State Advertisements (LSAs): OSPF routers exchange LSAs, which contain information about network topology. LSAs are used to build and maintain the link-state database.

Section 2: OSPF Area Types and Configuration

OSPF employs different area types to meet specific network requirements. Let's explore the common OSPF area types and their configuration:

Backbone Area (Area 0): The backbone area (Area 0) is the central area that connects all other areas in an OSPF network. It must be configured and defined before other areas can be added.

Standard Areas: Standard areas (non-backbone areas) are identified by area numbers other than 0. These areas connect to the backbone area and may contain routers and networks.

Stub Areas: Stub areas do not receive external routing information. They use a default route for external traffic and reduce routing table size. Configure a stub area using the "area <area number> stub" command.

Totally Stubby Areas: Totally stubby areas go a step further than stub areas by not allowing inter-area or external routes. They use a default route for all traffic. Configure a totally stubby area using the "area <area number> stub no-summary" command.

Section 3: OSPF Advanced Features and Optimization

OSPF provides advanced features and optimization techniques for improved performance. Let's explore some key aspects:

OSPF Cost: OSPF uses cost (metric) to calculate the path preference. By default, cost is based on interface bandwidth. Adjusting the cost can influence path selection. Use the "ip ospf cost" command under interface configuration mode.

OSPF Path Summarization: Path summarization can reduce the size of routing tables and improve network efficiency. Use the "area <area number> range" command to configure path summarization within an area.

Virtual Links: Virtual links establish logical connections between non-backbone areas through the backbone area. They are used when direct physical connections between areas are not possible.

Section 4: Troubleshooting OSPF Issues

Effective troubleshooting skills are crucial for network professionals. Let's explore common OSPF issues and their troubleshooting techniques:

Neighbor Adjacency Problems: If OSPF neighbors fail to form an adjacency, check that routers are in the same area, have compatible OSPF configurations, and are using the same network type (e.g., broadcast, point-to-point).

Inconsistent OSPF Databases: Inconsistent OSPF databases can occur due to synchronization issues between routers. Verify that routers have the same OSPF database, area ID, and LSA types.

Suboptimal Routing: Suboptimal routing can occur if OSPF path selection is not working as expected. Check OSPF costs, network topology, and verify that all routers have the same LSAs and routing information.

Route Redistribution: When redistributing routes from other routing protocols into OSPF or vice versa, ensure that redistribution configurations and filtering mechanisms are correctly set up. Verify redistribution statements and access-lists for any misconfigurations.

Section 5: OSPF Authentication and Security

To secure OSPF routing updates and prevent unauthorized access, authentication and security measures can be implemented. Here are key considerations:

OSPF Authentication: Enable OSPF authentication to authenticate OSPF routers within an area. Use the "ip ospf authentication" command under interface configuration mode to configure authentication.

Message Digest Algorithm 5 (MD5): OSPF supports MD5 authentication, which provides secure authentication between OSPF routers. Use the "ip ospf message-digest-key" command to configure MD5 authentication.

Section 6: Conclusion

In this chapter, we explored the implementation and management of OSPF. We covered OSPF basics, area types, configuration, advanced features, optimization techniques, troubleshooting, and security considerations. Understanding OSPF is crucial for success in the CCNP exam and real-world networking scenarios.

In the next chapter, we will delve into the implementation and management of BGP (Border Gateway Protocol), a critical routing protocol for connecting autonomous systems. We will cover BGP essentials, configuration, path selection, troubleshooting, and security aspects.

Chapter 5: Implementing and Managing BGP

Welcome to Chapter 5 of "Mastering the CCNP: A Comprehensive Exam Prep Guide." In this chapter, we will focus on Border Gateway Protocol (BGP), a crucial routing protocol for connecting autonomous systems. We will explore BGP essentials, configuration, path selection, troubleshooting, and security aspects. Let's dive in!

Section 1: BGP Essentials and Functions

BGP is an exterior gateway protocol used to exchange routing information between different autonomous systems (AS). Understanding the essentials of BGP is key to its implementation. Here are some important concepts:

Autonomous System (AS): An AS is a collection of networks under a single administrative domain. BGP uses AS numbers to uniquely identify autonomous systems.

BGP Peering: BGP routers establish peering relationships to exchange routing information. There are two types of peering: internal BGP (iBGP) for routers within the same AS and external BGP (eBGP) for routers in different ASes.

BGP Attributes: BGP uses various attributes to determine the best path for routing. Key attributes include the next hop, AS path, local preference, origin, and metrics like the MED (Multi-Exit Discriminator).

Section 2: BGP Neighbor Establishment and Peering

To exchange BGP routing information, routers need to establish neighbor relationships. Let's explore the steps to configure BGP neighbor peering:

Enable BGP: Enable BGP routing on a router using the "router bgp <AS number>" command in global configuration mode.

Establish Neighbor Relationships: Configure neighbor relationships using the "neighbor <IP address>" command under the router bgp configuration mode. Specify the remote router's IP address, AS number, and other peering parameters.

BGP Authentication: To secure BGP peering, enable authentication using the "neighbor <IP address> password <password>" command. Ensure that both routers have the same password configured.

Section 3: BGP Path Selection and Routing Policies

BGP uses path selection mechanisms to determine the best path for routing. Understanding path selection and configuring routing policies is essential. Let's cover some important aspects:

BGP Path Selection: BGP uses a set of criteria, known as the path selection process, to determine the best path. These criteria include the weight, local preference, AS path length, origin code, MED, and next hop.

BGP Route Maps: Route maps allow for the manipulation and control of BGP routing updates. They can be used to modify attributes, filter routes, set conditions, and apply routing policies. Use the "route-map" command under the router bgp or neighbor configuration mode to configure route maps.

BGP Community: BGP communities are tags used to group routes and define routing policies. They allow network administrators to influence the path selection process or apply specific policies to routes. Use the "community" command under the route-map configuration mode to configure BGP communities.

Section 4: Troubleshooting BGP Issues

Troubleshooting BGP issues requires a systematic approach. Let's explore common BGP issues and their troubleshooting techniques:

Neighbor Establishment Problems: If BGP neighbors fail to establish a connection, verify the IP address, AS number, and peering parameters configured on both routers. Check for network connectivity issues, authentication mismatches, and firewall rules.

Route Not Advertised: If a BGP route is not being advertised, ensure that the network is correctly defined using the "network" command under the router bgp configuration mode. Check for any route-map filters or redistribution issues.

Suboptimal Routing: BGP path selection determines the best route based on various attributes. Verify that the BGP attributes are configured correctly and that no route maps or filters are impacting the path selection process.

BGP Route Flapping: BGP route flapping occurs when a route frequently alternates between available and unavailable states. This can cause instability in the network. Investigate network connectivity, route instability, and potential misconfigurations.

Section 5: BGP Security and Best Practices

BGP security is crucial to prevent unauthorized access and mitigate potential threats. Let's explore some security considerations and best practices:

BGP Route Filtering: Apply inbound and outbound route filters using access control lists (ACLs) to filter unwanted or unauthorized routes. This helps protect against route hijacking and route leaks.

Route Validation: Implement mechanisms such as Resource Public Key Infrastructure (RPKI) to validate the authenticity of BGP routes. RPKI helps prevent the propagation of incorrect or malicious routing information.

BGP Session Security: Protect BGP sessions using secure protocols such as TCP Authentication Option (TCP-AO) or IPsec. These protocols ensure confidentiality, integrity, and authenticity of BGP communication.

Section 6: Conclusion

In this chapter, we explored the implementation and management of BGP. We covered BGP essentials, neighbor establishment and peering, path selection and routing policies, troubleshooting techniques, and security considerations. Understanding BGP is vital for both the CCNP exam and real-world networking scenarios.

In the next chapter, we will delve into the implementation and management of redistribution, a critical process for exchanging routing information between different routing protocols. We will cover redistribution basics, techniques, filtering, and troubleshooting aspects.

Chapter 6: Implementing and Managing Redistribution

Welcome to Chapter 6 of "Mastering the CCNP: A Comprehensive Exam Prep Guide." In this chapter, we will focus on redistribution, a crucial process for exchanging routing information between different routing protocols. We will explore redistribution basics, techniques, filtering, and troubleshooting aspects. Let's dive in!

Section 1: Understanding Redistribution

Redistribution enables routers to exchange routing information between different routing protocols, allowing networks to interoperate. Let's explore some important concepts:

Routing Protocol Interoperability: Different routing protocols use different metrics, administrative distances, and route selection processes. Redistribution allows for seamless communication between these protocols.

Redistribution Points: Redistribution points are routers where routing information is exchanged between different routing protocols. It is crucial to carefully select redistribution points to ensure proper routing behavior.

Section 2: Basic Redistribution Configuration

To implement redistribution, you need to configure redistribution statements on the appropriate routers. Let's cover the basic steps involved:

Identify Redistribution Points: Identify the routers where redistribution will be performed. These routers should have interfaces connected to networks that use different routing protocols.

Enable Redistribution: Use the appropriate command under the router configuration mode to enable redistribution for the desired routing protocol. For example, "redistribute ospf" enables redistribution of OSPF routes.

Specify the Target Protocol: Specify the routing protocol into which routes will be redistributed. Use the command "redistribute <source-protocol> into <target-protocol>" under the router configuration mode.

Fine-tuning Metrics: Optionally, you can manipulate metrics or administrative distances for redistributed routes using the appropriate commands. This can influence the selection of routes from the receiving protocol.

Section 3: Filtering and Route Redistribution

Filtering is an essential aspect of redistribution as it allows control over which routes are redistributed and which are not. Let's explore the filtering techniques:

Route Maps: Route maps provide flexible control over redistributed routes. You can use route maps to match specific conditions and filter routes based on criteria such as prefixes, metrics, tags, or access-lists. Configure route maps using the "route-map" command.

Distribute Lists: Distribute lists offer another way to filter redistributed routes. They are applied to an interface or routing process and control which routes are allowed or denied for redistribution. Use the "distribute-list" command to configure distribute lists.

Tagging and Filtering by Tags: Tagging routes can help identify specific routes for redistribution filtering. You can assign tags using route maps or distribute lists and filter routes based on their tags using the appropriate commands.

Section 4: Troubleshooting Redistribution Issues

Troubleshooting redistribution can be complex due to the interaction between different routing protocols. Let's explore some common issues and their troubleshooting techniques:

Incomplete Route Redistribution: If certain routes are not being redistributed as expected, check for correct redistribution configurations on the routers involved. Verify that network statements, redistribution statements, and filtering conditions are properly configured.

Route Instability: Redistribution can sometimes lead to route instability, causing frequent route flapping or suboptimal routing. Check for redistribution loops, incorrect metric settings, or routing protocol convergence issues.

Route Filtering Problems: If routes are not being filtered correctly during redistribution, double-check the filtering mechanisms in place. Verify that route maps, distribute lists, or tags are correctly configured and applied where necessary.

Redistribution Loops: Misconfigured redistribution can result in routing loops, where routes continuously bounce between different routing protocols. Ensure that redistribution points are carefully selected, and appropriate filtering conditions are set up to prevent loops.

Section 5: Conclusion

In this chapter, we explored the implementation and management of redistribution. We discussed redistribution basics, configuration steps, filtering techniques, and troubleshooting strategies. Understanding redistribution is crucial for network professionals, as it enables the seamless exchange of routing information between different protocols.

In the next chapter, we will delve into Quality of Service (QoS). We will discuss QoS principles, classification, marking, congestion management, and QoS mechanisms for voice and video traffic.

Chapter 7: Quality of Service (QoS)

Welcome to Chapter 7 of "Mastering the CCNP: A Comprehensive Exam Prep Guide." In this chapter, we will focus on Quality of Service (QoS), a critical aspect of network management that ensures reliable and predictable delivery of network traffic. We will explore QoS principles, traffic classification, marking, congestion management, and QoS mechanisms for voice and video traffic. Let's dive in!

Section 1: QoS Principles and Models

QoS principles provide the foundation for managing network traffic and ensuring optimal performance. Let's explore some key principles:

Bandwidth Management: QoS allows you to allocate and prioritize available bandwidth to different types of network traffic based on their importance and requirements.

Traffic Differentiation: QoS helps differentiate and prioritize network traffic based on its characteristics, such as application type, sensitivity, and latency requirements.

Congestion Management: QoS mechanisms assist in managing network congestion by prioritizing and controlling the flow of traffic during periods of high demand.

Section 2: Traffic Classification and Marking

Traffic classification is a vital step in implementing QoS. It involves identifying and categorizing different types of network traffic. Let's explore the process of traffic classification and marking:

Classification Criteria: Identify criteria for classifying traffic, such as source/destination IP addresses, port numbers, protocol types, or DiffServ Code Points (DSCP).

Classification Methods: Use various methods to classify traffic, including Access Control Lists (ACLs), Network-Based Application Recognition (NBAR), or Class-Based QoS (CBQoS) tools.

Traffic Marking: Once traffic is classified, it can be marked with specific values or tags that indicate its priority or treatment. Common methods include setting the IP Precedence or DSCP field in IP packet headers.

Section 3: Congestion Management and Avoidance

Congestion management and avoidance techniques help ensure efficient utilization of network resources and mitigate the effects of congestion. Let's explore some key mechanisms:

Queuing: Queuing mechanisms control the order in which packets are transmitted from congested interfaces. Popular queuing algorithms include First-In-First-Out (FIFO), Weighted Fair Queuing (WFQ), and Class-Based Queuing (CBQ).

Traffic Shaping: Traffic shaping controls the flow of network traffic by smoothing out bursts of data and enforcing specific traffic rates. Token Bucket and Generic Traffic Shaping (GTS) are common shaping techniques.

Congestion Avoidance: Congestion avoidance mechanisms, such as Random Early Detection (RED) or Weighted Random Early Detection (WRED), proactively drop or mark packets when network congestion is detected, preventing excessive queuing.

Section 4: QoS Mechanisms for Voice and Video

Voice and video traffic have stringent requirements for latency, jitter, and packet loss. QoS mechanisms ensure optimal performance for real-time communication. Let's explore key mechanisms for voice and video traffic:

Classification and Marking: Voice and video traffic can be classified and marked with high-priority values, such as EF (Expedited Forwarding), to ensure their preferential treatment throughout the network.

Low-Latency Queuing (LLQ): LLQ assigns strict priority to voice traffic, allowing it to bypass other types of traffic in the queue, ensuring low latency and minimal delay.

Quality of Service for Real-Time Protocol (QoS RTP): QoS RTP helps ensure proper treatment of Real-Time Transport Protocol (RTP) packets used for voice and video streaming. It includes mechanisms for prioritization, marking, and shaping.

Section 5: Conclusion

In this chapter, we explored Quality of Service (QoS) principles, traffic classification, marking, congestion management, and QoS mechanisms for voice and video traffic. Understanding QoS is crucial for optimizing network performance and delivering a high-quality user experience.

In the next chapter, we will focus on Wide Area Networks (WANs). We will explore WAN technologies such as HDLC, PPP, Frame Relay, Virtual Private Networks (VPNs), and Multiprotocol Label Switching (MPLS). We will discuss their features, configuration, and troubleshooting aspects.

Chapter 8: Wide Area Networks (WANs)

Welcome to Chapter 8 of "Mastering the CCNP: A Comprehensive Exam Prep Guide." In this chapter, we will explore Wide Area Networks (WANs) and their technologies. We will cover WAN basics, HDLC, PPP, Frame Relay, Virtual Private Networks (VPNs), and Multiprotocol Label Switching (MPLS). Let's dive in!

Section 1: Understanding Wide Area Networks (WANs)

WANs connect geographically dispersed locations and facilitate the transmission of data over long distances. Let's explore some key concepts related to WANs:

WAN Components: WANs typically consist of routers, switches, communication links, and service providers. They enable organizations to establish reliable connections between their remote sites.

WAN Technologies: Various technologies are used in WANs, including HDLC, PPP, Frame Relay, ATM, Ethernet WAN, MPLS, and VPNs. Each technology has its own characteristics, advantages, and use cases.

Section 2: HDLC (High-Level Data Link Control)

HDLC is a synchronous data link layer protocol commonly used in WAN environments. Let's explore HDLC and its features:

Point-to-Point Communication: HDLC is typically used in point-to-point connections between two devices, such as routers or switches.

Framing and Bit Stuffing: HDLC encapsulates data into frames, ensuring reliable transmission. Bit stuffing is used to maintain frame synchronization.

HDLC Operation Modes: HDLC supports three operation modes: Normal Response Mode (NRM), Asynchronous Balanced Mode (ABM), and Asynchronous Response Mode (ARM).

Section 3: PPP (Point-to-Point Protocol)

PPP is a widely used data link layer protocol for establishing and managing point-to-point connections. Let's explore PPP and its features:

Authentication and Encryption: PPP supports various authentication methods, including PAP (Password Authentication Protocol) and CHAP (Challenge Handshake Authentication Protocol). Encryption can be implemented using protocols like EAP (Extensible Authentication Protocol) or MPPE (Microsoft Point-to-Point Encryption).

Link Control Protocol (LCP): LCP is responsible for establishing, configuring, and terminating PPP connections. It negotiates authentication, compression, and IP address assignment.

Network Control Protocol (NCP): NCP allows the transmission of network layer protocols, such as IP, IPv6, IPX, or AppleTalk, over PPP connections. Each protocol has its own NCP for encapsulation and configuration.

Section 4: Frame Relay

Frame Relay is a packet-switched WAN technology that offers cost-effective connectivity for remote sites. Let's explore Frame Relay and its features:

Virtual Circuits: Frame Relay uses virtual circuits (VCs) to establish logical connections between sites. Permanent Virtual Circuits (PVCs) are preconfigured, while Switched Virtual Circuits (SVCs) are dynamically established.

DLCI (Data Link Connection Identifier): Frame Relay uses DLCIs to identify each virtual circuit within a network. DLCIs are locally significant and used for routing purposes.

Committed Information Rate (CIR): CIR specifies the guaranteed bandwidth allocated to a Frame Relay connection. Exceeding the CIR may result in discarding excess traffic.

Section 5: Virtual Private Networks (VPNs)

VPNs provide secure and private communication over public networks. Let's explore VPNs and their key components:

Tunneling: VPNs use tunneling protocols like IPsec (Internet Protocol Security) to encapsulate and encrypt data for secure transmission across public networks.

VPN Types: Common VPN types include Site-to-Site VPNs, which connect multiple remote sites, and Remote Access VPNs, which allow individual users to securely access the network remotely.

VPN Protocols: VPNs can be implemented using protocols such as IPsec, SSL/TLS (Secure Sockets Layer/Transport Layer Security), or PPTP (Point-to-Point Tunneling Protocol).

Section 6: Multiprotocol Label Switching (MPLS)

MPLS is a flexible WAN technology that improves the efficiency and performance of network traffic routing. Let's explore MPLS and its key characteristics:

Label Switching: MPLS uses labels to identify and forward network traffic. Labels are added to packets at the ingress router and switched along the MPLS network based on the forwarding table.

Traffic Engineering: MPLS enables traffic engineering by allowing network administrators to control the path and prioritize specific types of traffic based on QoS requirements.

MPLS VPNs: MPLS supports MPLS VPNs, which provide secure and scalable connectivity between different sites while maintaining isolation of customer traffic.

Section 7: Conclusion

In this chapter, we explored Wide Area Networks (WANs) and their technologies. We covered WAN basics, HDLC, PPP, Frame Relay, Virtual Private Networks (VPNs), and Multiprotocol Label Switching (MPLS). Understanding these technologies is crucial for managing and maintaining efficient communication across geographically dispersed sites.

In the next chapter, we will focus on network security. We will explore security threats, best practices for securing networks, firewall technologies, intrusion detection and prevention systems, and Virtual Private Networks (VPNs) for secure remote access.

Chapter 9: Network Security

Welcome to Chapter 9 of "Mastering the CCNP: A Comprehensive Exam Prep Guide." In this chapter, we will focus on network security, a critical aspect of modern networking. We will explore security threats, best practices for securing networks, firewall technologies, intrusion detection and prevention systems, and Virtual Private Networks (VPNs) for secure remote access. Let's dive in!

Section 1: Understanding Network Security

Network security aims to protect networks, devices, and data from unauthorized access, misuse, and malicious attacks. Let's explore some key concepts related to network security:

Security Threats: Network security threats include unauthorized access, data breaches, malware infections, denial of service attacks, social engineering, and more. Understanding these threats is essential for implementing effective security measures.

Defense in Depth: Defense in Depth is a security principle that involves implementing multiple layers of security controls to provide comprehensive protection. This includes physical security, network security, host security, application security, and user awareness.

Section 2: Best Practices for Network Security

Implementing best practices is crucial for maintaining a secure network environment. Let's explore some important network security best practices:

Access Control: Implement strong access control mechanisms, such as role-based access control (RBAC), to ensure that only authorized users can access network resources.

Strong Authentication: Use strong authentication methods, including multi-factor authentication (MFA) and secure password policies, to prevent unauthorized access.

Regular Patching and Updates: Keep network devices, operating systems, and applications up to date with the latest security patches and updates to address vulnerabilities.

Security Auditing and Monitoring: Regularly audit and monitor network activities to detect and respond to potential security breaches. Use security information and event management (SIEM) tools for centralized monitoring and analysis.

Section 3: Firewall Technologies

Firewalls play a crucial role in network security by enforcing access control policies and protecting against unauthorized access. Let's explore firewall technologies:

Network Firewalls: Network firewalls, such as stateful firewalls, inspect network traffic at the network layer (Layer 3) and enforce security policies based on source/destination IP addresses and port numbers.

Application Firewalls: Application firewalls operate at the application layer (Layer 7) and provide more granular control over network traffic, allowing inspection and filtering of specific application protocols.

Next-Generation Firewalls (NGFW): NGFWs combine traditional firewall functionality with advanced features such as intrusion prevention, deep packet inspection, and application awareness.

Section 4: Intrusion Detection and Prevention Systems (IDS/IPS)

Intrusion Detection Systems (IDS) and Intrusion Prevention Systems (IPS) are essential for detecting and mitigating security threats. Let's explore IDS/IPS technologies:

Intrusion Detection Systems (IDS): IDS monitors network traffic, analyzes it for suspicious patterns or behaviors, and generates alerts when potential threats are detected.

Intrusion Prevention Systems (IPS): IPS goes a step further by actively blocking or mitigating identified threats, providing real-time protection against attacks.

Signature-Based vs. Behavior-Based Detection: IDS/IPS can use signature-based detection, where known patterns or signatures of attacks are matched, or behavior-based detection, where abnormal network behavior is identified.

Section 5: Virtual Private Networks (VPNs) for Secure Remote Access

VPNs provide secure remote access to networks over public or untrusted networks such as the internet. Let's explore VPN technologies:

Site-to-Site VPN: Site-to-Site VPNs allow secure connectivity between geographically separated networks, providing a secure channel for communication.

Remote Access VPN: Remote Access VPNs enable individual users to securely access the network remotely, typically using encrypted tunnels and authentication mechanisms.

VPN Protocols: Common VPN protocols include IPsec (Internet Protocol Security), SSL/TLS (Secure Sockets Layer/Transport Layer Security), and OpenVPN.

Section 6: Conclusion

In this chapter, we explored network security and its various aspects. We discussed security threats, best practices for network security, firewall technologies, intrusion detection and prevention systems, and Virtual Private Networks (VPNs) for secure remote access. Understanding network security is crucial for protecting networks and data in an increasingly interconnected world.

In the next chapter, we will delve into network automation and programmability. We will explore software-defined networking (SDN), network automation tools, scripting languages, and infrastructure as code (IaC) concepts.

Chapter 10: Network Automation and Programmability

Welcome to Chapter 10 of "Mastering the CCNP: A Comprehensive Exam Prep Guide." In this chapter, we will explore network automation and programmability, essential skills for modern network engineers. We will discuss software-defined networking (SDN), network automation tools, scripting languages, and infrastructure as code (IaC) concepts. Let's dive in!

Section 1: Understanding Network Automation and Programmability

Network automation and programmability aim to simplify network management, improve operational efficiency, and enable rapid provisioning of network services. Let's explore some key concepts related to network automation and programmability:

Software-Defined Networking (SDN): SDN separates the control plane from the data plane, allowing network administrators to centrally manage and control the network using software-based controllers.

Programmable Networks: Programmable networks enable network engineers to automate repetitive tasks, dynamically configure network devices, and customize network behavior using programmable interfaces.

Infrastructure as Code (IaC): IaC is a concept where network configurations and deployments are managed through machine-readable code. This allows for consistent and automated provisioning of network resources.

Section 2: Network Automation Tools

Various tools and frameworks are available to facilitate network automation. Let's explore some popular network automation tools:

Ansible: Ansible is an open-source automation platform that simplifies network automation through declarative configuration management, task automation, and orchestration.

Puppet: Puppet is a configuration management tool that enables network administrators to define and manage network configurations through reusable manifests.

Chef: Chef is another configuration management tool that focuses on infrastructure automation. It allows for the creation of reusable cookbooks to define and manage network configurations.

Section 3: Scripting Languages for Network Automation

Scripting languages play a crucial role in network automation. Let's explore some commonly used scripting languages for network automation:

Python: Python is a versatile and widely used scripting language with a rich ecosystem of libraries and frameworks. It is well-suited for network automation tasks, such as device configuration, API interactions, and data parsing.

Bash: Bash (Bourne Again SHell) is a scripting language commonly used in Unix-based systems. It is useful for automating tasks at the command line interface (CLI) and executing system-level operations.

PowerShell: PowerShell is a scripting language primarily used in Windows environments. It provides extensive capabilities for automating network configurations and managing Windows-based network devices.

Section 4: Infrastructure as Code (IaC) and Configuration Management

Infrastructure as Code (IaC) allows for the automated provisioning and management of network infrastructure through code. Let's explore some key concepts related to IaC and configuration management:

Configuration Management Tools: Configuration management tools, such as Terraform and CloudFormation, enable the provisioning and management of network resources using declarative code.

Templates and Modules: IaC frameworks utilize templates and modules to define infrastructure configurations. Templates provide a blueprint for provisioning resources, while modules enable reusable and modular infrastructure components.

Version Control: Version control systems like Git play a crucial role in managing infrastructure code. They allow for tracking changes, collaborating with team members, and rolling back configurations if needed.

Section 5: SDN and Network Programmability

Software-Defined Networking (SDN) and network programmability enable network engineers to dynamically control and manage network behavior. Let's explore some key concepts related to SDN and network programmability:

SDN Controllers: SDN controllers provide a centralized management point for network configuration and control. They interact with network devices using protocols like OpenFlow to control the forwarding behavior.

APIs and Northbound Interfaces: APIs (Application Programming Interfaces) and northbound interfaces provide programmatic access to SDN controllers, allowing network engineers to customize and automate network configurations.

Network Automation and Orchestration: Network automation and orchestration frameworks, such as Cisco DNA Center and OpenStack, simplify the deployment and management of network services through programmable interfaces.

Section 6: Conclusion

In this chapter, we explored network automation and programmability. We discussed software-defined networking (SDN), network automation tools, scripting languages for network automation, and infrastructure as code (IaC) concepts. Network automation and programmability are critical skills for modern network engineers, enabling them to streamline operations and adapt to evolving network requirements.

In the next chapter, we will delve into network troubleshooting techniques. We will explore common network issues, diagnostic tools, network monitoring, and best practices for effective network troubleshooting.

Chapter 11: Network Troubleshooting Techniques

Welcome to Chapter 11 of "Mastering the CCNP: A Comprehensive Exam Prep Guide." In this chapter, we will focus on network troubleshooting techniques, an essential skill for network engineers. We will explore common network issues, diagnostic tools, network monitoring, and best practices for effective network troubleshooting. Let's dive in!

Section 1: Understanding Network Troubleshooting

Network troubleshooting is the process of identifying, diagnosing, and resolving network issues to ensure optimal network performance. Let's explore some key concepts related to network troubleshooting:

Troubleshooting Methodology: A systematic approach is crucial for efficient troubleshooting. Common troubleshooting methodologies include the OSI model-based approach, such as the "bottom-up" or "top-down" approach, and the "divide and conquer" approach.

Documentation and Baseline: Maintaining accurate network documentation and establishing a performance baseline help identify deviations and track changes when troubleshooting.

Section 2: Common Network Issues

Networks can experience various issues that impact performance and connectivity. Let's explore some common network issues:

Connectivity Problems: Connectivity issues can result from misconfigured devices, physical layer problems, IP addressing conflicts, or routing issues.

Slow Network Performance: Slow network performance can be caused by congestion, bandwidth limitations, misconfigured devices, or excessive network traffic.

Packet Loss and Latency: Packet loss and latency can be caused by network congestion, high utilization, transmission errors, or network configuration problems.

Section 3: Diagnostic Tools for Network Troubleshooting

Diagnostic tools assist network engineers in identifying and resolving network issues. Let's explore some common diagnostic tools:

Ping: The ping utility is used to test connectivity between devices by sending ICMP Echo Request messages and receiving Echo Reply messages. It helps identify network reachability and latency issues.

Traceroute: Traceroute provides information about the path packets take from a source to a destination, showing the routers traversed along the way. It helps identify network latency and routing issues.

Network Analyzers: Network analyzers, such as Wireshark, capture and analyze network traffic at the packet level. They help identify packet loss, latency, and protocol-specific issues.

Section 4: Network Monitoring and Management

Network monitoring plays a crucial role in identifying and preventing network issues. Let's explore some key aspects of network monitoring and management:

SNMP (Simple Network Management Protocol): SNMP enables the monitoring and management of network devices by collecting and reporting data about device health, performance, and utilization.

Syslog: Syslog is a standard protocol for message logging, allowing network devices to send log messages to a central server for monitoring and troubleshooting.

Network Management Systems (NMS): NMS tools, such as Nagios, Zabbix, or SolarWinds, provide centralized

monitoring, alerting, and management capabilities for
networks.

Section 5: Best Practices for Effective Network Troubleshooting

Following best practices helps ensure efficient and effective
network troubleshooting. Let's explore some best practices
for network troubleshooting:

Gather Information: Gather relevant information about the
reported issue, including symptoms, affected devices, recent
changes, and any error messages or logs.

Use the Right Tools: Select and utilize appropriate diagnostic
tools to identify and isolate network issues. Ping, traceroute,
network analyzers, and logging tools can provide valuable
insights.

Divide and Conquer: Break down complex network issues
into smaller parts and systematically eliminate potential
causes. Isolate specific areas, devices, or protocols to narrow
down the scope of troubleshooting.

Document and Test: Document troubleshooting steps,
changes made, and their outcomes. Test the network after
implementing changes to verify the resolution of the issue.

Section 6: Conclusion

In this chapter, we explored network troubleshooting techniques. We discussed common network issues, diagnostic tools, network monitoring, and best practices for effective network troubleshooting. Network troubleshooting is a critical skill for network engineers, enabling them to identify and resolve network issues promptly, ensuring optimal network performance.

In the next chapter, we will focus on network design principles. We will explore network design methodologies, network topology considerations, scalability, redundancy, and high availability concepts for designing robust and efficient networks.

Chapter 12: Network Design Principles

Welcome to Chapter 12 of "Mastering the CCNP: A Comprehensive Exam Prep Guide." In this chapter, we will focus on network design principles, a crucial aspect of network engineering. We will explore network design methodologies, network topology considerations, scalability, redundancy, and high availability concepts for designing robust and efficient networks. Let's dive in!

Section 1: Understanding Network Design

Network design involves creating a blueprint for building a network infrastructure that meets specific requirements and objectives. Let's explore some key concepts related to network design:

Design Methodologies: Various design methodologies, such as the Cisco Enterprise Architecture model or the OSI model-based approach, provide frameworks for network design.

Design Requirements: Design requirements include factors such as scalability, reliability, security, performance, and budget constraints. Understanding these requirements is crucial for creating an effective network design.

Section 2: Network Topology Considerations

Choosing the right network topology is essential for a well-designed network. Let's explore some key considerations for network topologies:

Physical Topologies: Physical topologies determine how network devices are physically connected. Common physical topologies include star, bus, ring, mesh, and hybrid topologies.

Logical Topologies: Logical topologies define how data flows within a network. Common logical topologies include the client-server model, peer-to-peer model, and hierarchical models like the three-tier architecture.

Scalability: Scalability refers to the ability of a network to accommodate growth and increased demand. Network topologies should be designed with scalability in mind to handle future expansion.

Section 3: Redundancy and High Availability

Redundancy and high availability are crucial for minimizing network downtime and ensuring continuous operation. Let's explore some concepts related to redundancy and high availability:

Redundant Links: Redundant links provide alternative paths in case of link failures. Implementing link redundancy through techniques like link aggregation or Spanning Tree Protocol (STP) helps ensure network resilience.

Redundant Devices: Redundant devices, such as redundant switches or routers, provide backup capabilities in case of device failures. Implementing protocols like Hot Standby Router Protocol (HSRP) or Virtual Router Redundancy Protocol (VRRP) enables seamless failover.

Load Balancing: Load balancing distributes network traffic across multiple paths or devices, optimizing resource utilization and preventing network congestion. Techniques like Equal-Cost Multipath (ECMP) or Link Aggregation Control Protocol (LACP) enable load balancing.

Section 4: Scalability and Capacity Planning

Scalability and capacity planning are essential for designing networks that can handle increasing demands. Let's explore some considerations for scalability and capacity planning:

Future Growth: Design networks with future growth in mind, considering factors such as increasing user demands, new applications, or potential mergers/acquisitions.

Bandwidth Planning: Estimate the required bandwidth for different network segments based on current and projected traffic patterns. Consider factors like peak usage, latency requirements, and QoS needs.

Network Segmentation: Segmenting the network into smaller, manageable subnets or virtual LANs (VLANs) enables efficient resource allocation and scalability.

Section 5: Security in Network Design

Network design should incorporate security measures to protect against unauthorized access and data breaches. Let's explore some security considerations in network design:

Defense in Depth: Implement multiple layers of security controls, such as firewalls, intrusion detection and prevention systems, access controls, and encryption, to provide comprehensive security.

Segmentation and Access Control: Use network segmentation and access control mechanisms, such as VLANs, ACLs, and secure network zones, to isolate critical resources and control traffic flow.

Network Monitoring: Implement network monitoring and logging systems to detect and respond to security incidents promptly. Network monitoring tools like IDS/IPS or SIEM solutions help monitor and analyze network traffic.

Section 6: Conclusion

In this chapter, we explored network design principles. We discussed network design methodologies, network topology considerations, scalability, redundancy, high availability concepts, and security considerations. Network design is crucial for creating efficient, resilient, and secure networks that meet specific requirements.

In the next chapter, we will focus on emerging technologies and trends in networking. We will explore concepts such as Software-Defined Networking (SDN), Network Functions Virtualization (NFV), Internet of Things (IoT), and Cloud Computing, and their impact on network architecture and management.

Chapter 13: Emerging Technologies in Networking

Welcome to Chapter 13 of "Mastering the CCNP: A Comprehensive Exam Prep Guide." In this chapter, we will explore emerging technologies in networking. We will delve into concepts such as Software-Defined Networking (SDN), Network Functions Virtualization (NFV), Internet of Things (IoT), and Cloud Computing. We will discuss their impact on network architecture, management, and the future of networking. Let's dive in!

Section 1: Software-Defined Networking (SDN)

Software-Defined Networking (SDN) revolutionizes traditional network architectures by decoupling the control plane from the data plane. Let's explore SDN and its key concepts:

SDN Architecture: SDN architecture consists of three layers: the Application Layer, the Control Layer, and the Infrastructure Layer. The Control Layer, managed by an SDN controller, centrally controls and manages network behavior.

Programmability and Automation: SDN enables network programmability, allowing network administrators to dynamically configure and control network devices using software-based controllers. Automation capabilities simplify network management and provisioning.

OpenFlow Protocol: The OpenFlow protocol is commonly used in SDN environments to communicate between the SDN controller and network devices. It provides instructions for traffic forwarding and allows centralized network control.

Section 2: Network Functions Virtualization (NFV)

Network Functions Virtualization (NFV) aims to virtualize and consolidate network functions into software-based instances. Let's explore NFV and its key concepts:

Virtualized Network Functions (VNFs): VNFs are software-based instances that replace traditional hardware-based network appliances, such as firewalls, routers, or load balancers. They provide network services and functionalities in a flexible and scalable manner.

Resource Pooling and Orchestration: NFV utilizes resource pooling, where virtualized network resources are dynamically allocated to meet network service requirements. Orchestration platforms manage the lifecycle of VNFs and automate deployment, scaling, and service chaining.

Benefits of NFV: NFV offers benefits such as cost reduction, flexibility, scalability, and rapid deployment of network services. It allows network operators to efficiently manage network resources and adapt to changing demands.

Section 3: Internet of Things (IoT) and Networking

The Internet of Things (IoT) refers to the network of interconnected devices and sensors that collect and exchange data. Let's explore IoT and its impact on networking:

Device Proliferation: IoT brings a massive proliferation of connected devices, requiring scalable network architectures to handle the increased number of endpoints and the volume of data they generate.

Communication Protocols: IoT devices use various communication protocols, such as MQTT, CoAP, or HTTP, to transmit data. Network engineers must be familiar with these protocols and ensure network compatibility.

Security Challenges: IoT introduces unique security challenges due to the large number of devices and potential vulnerabilities. Network security measures should include device authentication, data encryption, and access control to mitigate IoT-related threats.

Section 4: Cloud Computing and Networking

Cloud Computing has transformed the way organizations deploy and manage IT resources. Let's explore the impact of cloud computing on networking:

Virtual Private Clouds (VPCs): VPCs provide isolated virtual network environments within cloud platforms, enabling organizations to define their network topologies, subnets, and connectivity within the cloud.

Software-Defined Wide Area Networking (SD-WAN): SD-WAN leverages the cloud to simplify and optimize wide area network connectivity. It provides centralized control and management of WAN connections, improving performance and reducing costs.

Hybrid and Multi-Cloud Networking: Hybrid and multi-cloud environments require robust networking solutions to connect and manage resources across multiple cloud providers and on-premises infrastructure. Network engineers should be familiar with technologies like Virtual Private Networks (VPNs) and interconnectivity options.

Section 5: The Future of Networking

Emerging technologies continue to shape the future of networking. Let's explore some trends and predictions:

Intent-Based Networking (IBN): IBN aims to simplify network management by enabling administrators to define high-level intentions rather than configuring individual devices. Network automation, machine learning, and artificial intelligence play a crucial role in IBN.

5G and Network Convergence: The deployment of 5G networks and the convergence of network technologies, such as mobile networks, IoT, and fixed networks, will reshape network architectures and provide new opportunities for innovative services.

Network Security Evolution: As networks become more complex and threats evolve, network security will continue to advance. Technologies such as machine learning, behavioral analytics, and threat intelligence will play a vital role in network security.

Section 6: Conclusion

In this chapter, we explored emerging technologies in networking. We discussed Software-Defined Networking (SDN), Network Functions Virtualization (NFV), Internet of Things (IoT), and Cloud Computing. Understanding these technologies is crucial for network engineers to stay ahead in the ever-evolving networking landscape.

In the final chapter, we will summarize key concepts covered throughout the book and provide exam preparation tips to help you succeed in the CCNP certification exam.

Chapter 14: Exam Preparation and Tips

Welcome to Chapter 14, the final chapter of "Mastering the CCNP: A Comprehensive Exam Prep Guide." In this chapter, we will provide you with exam preparation tips and strategies to help you succeed in the CCNP certification exam. Let's dive in!

Section 1: Understanding the CCNP Certification Exam

The CCNP certification exam tests your knowledge and skills in advanced networking topics. It is essential to understand the exam structure and requirements. Let's explore some key aspects of the CCNP certification exam:

Exam Format: The CCNP exam typically consists of multiple-choice questions, simulations, and hands-on lab exercises that assess your theoretical knowledge and practical skills.

Exam Topics: Familiarize yourself with the exam topics outlined by Cisco. Ensure you have a solid understanding of all the covered domains, including routing protocols, network security, troubleshooting, and emerging technologies.

Exam Preparation Time: Allocate sufficient time for exam preparation based on your current knowledge and experience level. Consider creating a study schedule to help you stay organized and cover all the exam objectives.

Section 2: Study Resources and Materials

Having access to quality study resources and materials is crucial for effective exam preparation. Let's explore some recommended resources:

Official Cisco Documentation: Cisco provides official documentation, including configuration guides, command references, and whitepapers, which are valuable sources of information. Familiarize yourself with Cisco's documentation library.

Cisco Press Books: Cisco Press offers a wide range of study guides and reference books specifically designed for Cisco certifications. These books provide in-depth coverage of exam topics and can serve as a comprehensive study resource.

Online Learning Platforms: Explore online learning platforms that offer CCNP training courses, practice exams, and interactive study materials. These platforms provide a structured learning experience and can help reinforce your understanding of exam topics.

Section 3: Hands-on Practice and Lab Exercises

Hands-on practice is essential to solidify your understanding of networking concepts and to prepare for the practical aspects of the CCNP exam. Let's explore some hands-on practice strategies:

Set up a Lab Environment: Create a lab environment using network simulation software, such as Cisco Packet Tracer or GNS3. Practice configuring network devices, implementing protocols, and troubleshooting common network issues.

Complete Lab Exercises: Work through lab exercises provided in study guides or online resources. These exercises simulate real-world scenarios and allow you to apply your knowledge and skills in a practical setting.

Virtual Labs and Online Resources: Utilize virtual lab environments and online resources that offer interactive networking exercises and virtualized equipment. These platforms provide hands-on practice opportunities without the need for physical hardware.

Section 4: Practice Exams and Self-Assessment

Practice exams are an excellent way to assess your readiness for the CCNP certification exam and identify areas that require further study. Let's explore some self-assessment strategies:

Official Cisco Practice Exams: Cisco offers official practice exams that simulate the format and difficulty level of the actual certification exam. Take advantage of these practice exams to familiarize yourself with the question types and assess your knowledge.

Third-Party Practice Exams: Explore reputable third-party resources that provide CCNP practice exams. These practice exams can offer additional perspectives and help you gauge your exam readiness.

Identify Knowledge Gaps: Analyze the results of your practice exams to identify areas where you need further study. Focus your efforts on strengthening your knowledge in these specific domains.

Section 5: Exam-Day Strategies

On the day of the exam, it's important to be prepared and employ effective strategies to maximize your chances of success. Let's explore some exam-day strategies:

Read and Understand the Questions: Take the time to read each question carefully and ensure you understand what is being asked. Pay attention to keywords and specific details to choose the most appropriate answer.

Time Management: Allocate your time wisely during the exam. Answer the easier questions first and flag more challenging ones for review later. Use the remaining time to revisit flagged questions and double-check your answers.

Stay Calm and Focused: Maintaining a calm and focused mindset during the exam is crucial. Take deep breaths if you feel stressed and focus on each question one at a time.

Section 6: Post-Exam Analysis and Continuous Learning

After completing the exam, it's essential to analyze your performance and continue your learning journey. Let's explore some post-exam strategies:

Analyze Your Results: Evaluate your exam results and identify areas where you performed well and areas that need improvement. This analysis will guide your future learning efforts.

Continuous Learning: Networking technologies and best practices evolve over time. Stay updated with the latest industry trends, new technologies, and Cisco announcements to ensure your skills remain relevant.

Pursue Advanced Certifications: Consider pursuing advanced certifications, such as the Cisco Certified Internetwork Expert (CCIE), to further enhance your expertise and career prospects.

Section 7: Conclusion

Congratulations! You have completed the final chapter on exam preparation and tips. By following the strategies outlined in this chapter, you are well-equipped to tackle the CCNP certification exam with confidence. Remember to utilize quality study resources, engage in hands-on practice, and employ effective exam-day strategies. Best of luck in your CCNP certification journey!

Now that you have mastered the CCNP exam topics and exam preparation, the key to success lies in your hands. Go forth with confidence and build a rewarding career as a skilled and certified network professional.

www.ingramcontent.com/pod-product-compliance
Lightning Source LLC
LaVergne TN
LVHW051609050326
832903LV00033B/4422